Bioethics Matters

Dr. Moira McQueen

Bioethics Matters

A Guide for Concerned Catholics

burns & oates

Published by Burns & Oates, a Continuum imprint

The Tower Building   80 Maiden Lane
11 York Road   Suite 704
London   New York
SE1 7NX   NY 10038

www.continuumbooks.com

First published 2009

ISBN 978-08264-3510-1

Printed in the United Kingdom by Antony Rowe, Wiltshire

Contents

Part 2: Reproductive technologies

Part 3: End-of-life issues

Part 4: Catholic teaching on living life until the end

Introduction

Bioethics Matters is designed to inform and educate Catholics about vital topics in bioethics. These matters often call for detailed knowledge of Catholic teaching, but many of us do not know enough about what that teaching says on these kinds of issues. We want to know more about that teaching when we are making moral decisions in these areas, for good conscience decisions call for good information.

Lay people deserve to be as educated as possible in Catholic teaching. It is to the Church's advantage that they be educated in this area, in light of the laity's religious and civic responsibilities. Many of the burning issues of our times are bioethical: stem cell experimentation, euthanasia, and prenatal genetic diagnosis are only a few of the topics we read about in the newspaper or hear about on TV. It can be difficult to keep up to date with developments in these areas, as well as to stay informed about church teaching. This book can help Catholics navigate these pressing issues.

The book, which is divided into four parts, leads us from beginning-of-life to end-of-life questions, explaining specific Catholic teachings for each and offering examples of real-life cases. It acknowledges the prime importance of Roman Catholic magisterial teaching—that is, the official teachings of the popes and bishops—but references other documents and relevant material as well. Bioethics is a rapidly developing area; scientific breakthroughs and new discoveries are happening all the time. Readers are urged to keep studying and discussing bioethical issues in their parishes and homes.

Part 1:

Bioethics from a Roman Catholic perspective

1. What is ethics?

Ethics is a systematic way of thinking that provides a coherent set of values and principles to guide people's moral lives.

All people, whether they have thought this through or not, have a personal moral code. It is shaped by everything they have learned about human behaviour from many sources, including their own experience. This code is not always consistent. For example, people may fight for human rights, yet support choice in abortion, which denies the most fundamental of human rights. There is an "ought" or "duty" built into this moral code, regardless of whether people actually live up to it on all occasions.

The Catholic Church has its own distinctive body of ethical teaching, usually referred to as moral theology. It has been discerned over the centuries and is rooted in Scripture and natural law (moral principles that do not change and that are common to all people because they are human beings). We know from Scripture that the Christian is called to love, based on the Great Commandment Jesus gave us when someone asked him, "Which commandment is the first of all?" He replied, "The first is, 'Hear, O Israel:

the Lord our God, the Lord is one; you shall love the Lord your God with all your heart, and with all your soul, and with all your mind, and with all your strength.' The second is this, 'You shall love your neighbour as yourself.' There is no other commandment greater than these" (Mark 12:29-31).

If we take these two commandments seriously, we spend most of our moral life developing ways of giving meaning to them through our actions.

2. Some key terms

There are many types of ethical theory, with varying approaches to how one should think ethically and so make correct moral decisions. The following are some examples of these theories (or systems).

Duty-based ethics (deontology)

I act out of a sense of duty: I do what I think I *ought* to do; I do not do what I think I *ought not* do.

My duty arises from some law imposed on me; it is not determined by circumstances, and the consequences of my action are not mine to consider.

Example

> A priest or other moral adviser insists on a particular course of action as required by authority, such as not using contraception, without considering either the individual's circumstances or capacity to fulfill the law. The priest or adviser has done his or her duty, and therefore acted morally correctly, no matter what the consequences for the individual may be.

Goal-directed ethics (teleology)

I know what I want to achieve—that is, I have a goal or end in mind—and the purpose of my proposed plan of action is to achieve that goal. Consequently, the means I adopt to achieve my goal will be morally permissible. In fact, the given situation will determine what means are permissible.

Example

> A husband and wife wish to become parents but are having difficulty conceiving. There are various means to achieve this goal, which is a praiseworthy one. The couple could try to determine through natural means when in the woman's monthly cycle she is most likely to conceive. Or they could undergo medical tests to see whether there is a

physical problem that can be fixed. Or they could apply for in vitro fertilization, either using their own gametes or someone else's. Not all of these means are morally acceptable, as we will see in Part 2 of this book.

The greatest good for the greatest number of people (utilitarianism)

This system of ethics is based on maximizing the happiness or good of the greatest number of people through a given course of action. Those who use this approach must define *happiness* or *good* themselves.

Example

It is claimed by some medical authorities that all girls as young as twelve would benefit from being vaccinated against Human Papilloma Virus (HPV). This virus is transmitted through sexual intercourse and is known to cause some, but not all, cases of cervical cancer, which can be fatal.

Some legislatures have made the vaccine available through school boards, but Catholic school authorities know that church teaching requires abstinence from sexual intercourse before marriage. Apart from some questions about the vaccine's effectiveness, they will encounter some ethical difficulties in maintaining an ethos of abstinence, while promoting actions that assume that girls will inevitably be involved in premarital sex from an early age. What may be seen as "the greatest good" by other authorities raises different questions for Catholic values.

Consequentialism or pragmatism

This theory focuses exclusively on the good I want to gain and gives no weight to the morality of the way I achieve it. This is what people mean by "the end justifies the means." I simply disregard the fact that the means may be evil, because they achieve the end or goal that I seek. Alternatively, I regret having to use this particular means, but the goal demands it.

Example

President Truman wanted to end the Second World War. He knew that using the atomic bomb on cities in Japan would cause almost immediate surrender. And he reckoned that the number of civilians killed would be far fewer than the number killed through continued warfare. That innocent citizens were to be bombed was no deterrent; indeed, their deaths would save other lives.

Relativism

This is perhaps the most common ethical approach today. This theory takes the form of "you have your ideas and I have mine," and so it does not matter whether the same ideas lead different people to different conclusions. This approach lacks logic. It is impossible for two completely different views to be right at the same time.

Example

> One young woman thinks sex before marriage is a good idea, while another thinks there is merit in waiting until marriage. They both think they are right, but their views conflict. Relativism claims that there is no objective standard whereby one view may be judged morally correct, the other morally wrong. Individual choice is based on what is "good" for the individual.

Virtue ethics

This is not the same thing as an ethics of virtue, which is necessary in any moral theory. The latter examines the different moral virtues, and is sometimes termed an "ethics of becoming". Virtue ethics, on the other hand, claims to be a normative ethics. There is some justification for this, to the extent that what Aquinas would call connaturality with the good points us in the right direction. In a sense, as normative, virtue ethics is a back-to-front ethics. In other words, it is more logical to find the answer to a moral question and then check that this is in conformity with what a virtuous person would choose rather than propose, without logical process, to point to what a virtuous person would choose.

For example, if a woman has a degenerative disease, which will leave her progressively dependent on a care-giver, and will eventually result in her drawn-out death, how would virtue ethics decide whether euthanasia may be ethically allowable in this case? Would her sincere appreciation of the value of life mean she would reject any notion of euthanasia? That would be true only if her appreciation of life is absolute. If she sees exceptions to the prohibition against killing, she may see euthanasia in her own case as justifiable. To make the correct moral choice in this case, she needs the aid of further moral reasoning and the virtue to be open to such reasoning. Moral reasoning will lead her to understand that only God has dominion over human life and that the mystery of life makes deliberately ending it a choice beyond our human capacity to make. It will also lead her to consider what euthanasia will mean to society generally and to all who work with the dying.

Natural law

We experience and recognize that human beings have innate instincts and drives that direct them towards good and towards behaviour that realizes that good. Human reason helps us work out which behaviour does or does not promote human good. Catholic teaching has a long tradition that emphasizes the validity of human reason working with human experience to tell us what is best for human beings.

St. Thomas Aquinas wrote extensively in the thirteenth century on the moral life, which he inserted into the whole of Catholic doctrine. We are still indebted to him for showing us a model of reason enlightened by faith. We use reason when we think about issues, but, as Christian thinkers, our reason is open to direction from the Word of God.

Example

We have a drive to propagate. Reason and experience teach us that the best set of circumstances for conceiving and raising children is within the permanent and exclusive personal relationship of a man and a woman formed through the covenant of marriage. Scripture enlightens this rational conclusion with teaching about the relationship between Christ and his Church, about self-sacrificing love, about the human individual as the image of God and redeemed by Christ, and about sacramental grace.

Summary

The most common ethical theories are described briefly above. We can see the inadequacies of many of them. Natural law is in a class by itself, because it is the time-tested ethical approach used by the Catholic Church.

3. The human person

When, as Catholics, we talk about the human person, we are describing a unified entity made up of body, mind and spirit. We do not hold, for example, that the essential person is a soul trapped in a body. We share in God's nature here on earth, since God created us as intelligent, free beings. In heaven, we will experience the fullness of this sharing in the life of

God, who is love. We recognize our spiritual dimension: the desire we feel to reach out to the God who reaches out to us, the God to whom we pray and in whom we place our trust.

Scripture tells us that we are made in God's image (Genesis 1:26). We have heard this phrase so often that we may scarcely pay attention to it. When we stop to reflect, though, we realize that this is an amazing state of affairs. God has made us so we can share in the attributes that exist in God, such as love, goodness, mercy, truth and justice.

Our total selves are made in God's image. This realization helps us to appreciate the great gift of our physical selves, the bodies we use to communicate with each other in so many ways. Genesis continues, "male and female he created them" (Genesis 1:27). From this statement we conclude that "the unity of man and woman," as Pope John Paul II called it, is the way we live out God's purpose for us.[1]

In *Communion and Stewardship: Human Persons Created in the Image of God*, the International Theological Commission tells us that the whole of the person is created in God's image, including our reason and our sexuality.[2] We exist in relation to others, God and the world. We are essentially relational beings, not just isolated individuals.

The Commission said, "… human persons are created in the image of God in order to enjoy personal communion with the Father, Son and Holy Spirit and with one another in them, and in order to exercise, in God's name, responsible stewardship of the created world."[3]

The Commission wrote that the theology of the *imago dei* (image of God) links anthropology with moral theology by showing that the human person participates in the divine law through his or her being. The document refers to communion and stewardship because it is this likeness to the Trinity that makes the communion of created beings with the uncreated persons of the Trinity even possible. We are "by nature bodily and spiritual, men and women made for one another, persons oriented towards communion with God and one another, wounded by sin and in need of salvation, and destined to be conformed to Christ, the perfect image of the Father, in the power of the Holy Spirit."[4]

As Christians, we also think of our being as part of the Body of Christ. St. Paul developed his theology of the Christian community around this theme, and we use this to describe our membership in the Church. We know that what we do, for good or ill, affects the whole Christian body and, in fact, society as a whole.

We have a true, not abstract, social responsibility for each other flowing from our membership in the Body of Christ. We emphasize the human person, but not simply as an individual: the Church has always insisted on the importance of our contributing to the common good, reflecting both our civic and religious responsibilities.

Being made in God's image has many implications. Most importantly, it is the foundation of our human dignity. If every one of us is made in God's image, then every one of us is important, regardless of age, sex, creed or race.

Example

A human embryo must be protected because it is alive, just as a sick person must be protected from unethical interventions or neglect. This basic equality of persons is absolute, though many deny it. It is the basis on which the Catholic Church rests its whole teaching on respect for human life from conception until natural death.

4. Sources of Roman Catholic ethics: Revelation and natural law

Catholics have two main sources to consult when informing their conscience and making moral decisions: revelation (Scripture) and natural law.

The role of Scripture

The Catholic Church does not subscribe to the concept of *sola scriptura*, according to which the only legitimate moral principles are those found in Scripture.

The preferred approach to Scripture is complex and sophisticated, and cannot be reduced to simply reading the Bible. Instead, any study of Scripture should feature four aspects to help prevent readers from drawing conclusions in a fundamentalist way: exegesis, hermeneutics, methodology and theology.

Exegesis

Exegesis involves trying to decipher the meaning of the text in its original context. We must remember that the scriptural canon (the books of the Bible that the Church recognizes as inspired by God), although written by humans, are inspired by the Spirit, which is why we treat Scripture with due reverence. At the same time, we recognize that humans live in specific time periods and as such are affected by the culture of their time and by history. This means that we have to understand the context in which the text was written, including the historical circumstances, the language used and the socio-economic circumstances. Since we are far removed from the time the Scripture was written, and few of us know and understand the language the authors wrote in, we cannot be sure we are saying or meaning the same thing as they did, even when we use the same terms.

Hermeneutics

After considering Scripture in the context in which it was written, we must then try to establish the meaning of the text for today. This is known as hermeneutics. It is not an easy task, even for those who are skilled at it. When we read Scripture, we automatically interpret it through our own situation. We have new questions to ask of Scripture because we have had a different set of experiences. Once we become aware that this is what we are doing, we realize that this approach may distort the original meaning.

Hermeneutics shows us that we have to be careful how we interpret Scripture. We certainly cannot interpret it literally, at face value. The texts contain assumptions, and we approach the texts with our own assumptions. This means that we filter the texts through our own symbols, icons, language and values, which are clearly different from those of the times in which Scripture was written. Moral theologian and author Richard Gula warns us against "uncritical" use of Scripture, whereby we do not meet the challenge of interpreting the text and do not take seriously the difference between then and now.[5]

Methodology

There are different ways of using Scripture for moral guidance. The way we use it is closely tied to how we view moral theology. Gula notes that if we see moral theology as mainly being concerned about actions and decision making, then we will probably pay close attention to biblical imperatives: what we should and should not do. If, however, we are more attuned to finding out what sort of people we should be, we are more likely to look at parables and stories.

James M. Gustafson describes these two approaches as "revealed morality" and "revealed reality."[6] The former tends toward specific guidance, while the latter sheds light on how we can respond to situations based on the Gospel values of love, justice, peace and so on, as modelled by Jesus and the early Christians. Put together, these two approaches, or methods, help to inform our conscience about what to do and how to do it.

Theology

Before we can turn to Scripture for moral guidance, we must reconcile the Bible with thinking that is based on natural law. Historically, as moral theology became a separate discipline, it moved further away from Scripture and relied more on reason and logic.

The Second Vatican Council charged moral theologians with the task of integrating Scripture with natural law–based thinking to represent more fully the claims of "faith seeking understanding," in St. Augustine's famous phrase.[7] Moral theology at that time, in the early to mid-1960s, was moving from focusing mainly on evaluating particular actions to being concerned with human flourishing. The directive from the Second Vatican Council was welcomed as a more adequate way of discussing the rightness or wrongness of human behaviour, by demanding a search for a fuller understanding of what it means to be a person. This search must be undertaken in the wider context of what it means to be a Christian: a disciple not of the Church and its moral theology, but of Jesus Christ.

The role of natural law

The natural law–based approach acknowledges the capability of reason, reflecting on experience, to reach valid ethical conclusions.

This approach fits with the reminder given to us in *Gaudium et Spes* (The Church in the Modern World),[8] an important document of the Second Vatican Council, that we must become aware of and attentive to "the signs of the times" (4). This means that we are to be aware of current social, political and economic realities and, informed as much as possible about them, make our moral decisions "in light of the Gospel."

Becoming aware of the signs of the times requires a natural law–based approach, one that has a long-standing tradition in moral theology. Why has the Catholic Church relied on this method for its moral reasoning down through the ages? The answer is partly that Catholic theology has always tried to fit with the natural human desire to seek explanations, which we must see as making sense.

As humans, we examine arguments for and against all sorts of concepts. We base our arguments on evidence of some kind and expect to be shown facts that back them up. We require proof from people before we rely on their judgments or statements, at least until we know that their word is reliable. This does not make us all "doubting Thomases"; rather, it is part of our inclination to seek the truth and our ability to recognize the truth when we see it. Natural law is natural, then, in the sense of being part of our basic human nature. We have intelligence to see the logic of some positions and we have judgment based on experience to guide us to conclusions.

From the early church Fathers, through to St. Augustine and St. Thomas Aquinas, the Catholic Church has presented intellectually sound and intricate explanations of what is entailed in living the Christian life. Aquinas is famous for integrating Christian thought with the work of Aristotle, the great philosopher. In so doing, Aquinas strengthened the Church's position on the *understanding* part of "faith seeking understanding," by giving philosophical backbone to theological questions.

This natural law–based approach is of immense importance in our world because it enables Roman Catholics to become involved in ethical debates with people from any or no religious tradition. We do not rely only on Scripture to *prove* the points we are making. We recognize that people of other traditions also want to hear cogent, logical explanations of these points; we must strive to make sure that our statements are structured in such a way.

This does no injustice to our faith stance; rather, realizing that our faith stance is not universally accepted, we must use other ways of persuading people of the rightness of our moral arguments. For those of us within the Church, of course, the importance of revelation cannot be overemphasized.

Pope Pius XII spoke of this in his 1950 encyclical *Humani Generis* (Concerning Some False Opinions Threatening to Undermine the Foundations of Catholic Doctrine)[9]:

> … For though, absolutely speaking, human
> reason by its own natural force and light
> can arrive at a true and certain knowledge

of the one personal God, Who by His providence watches over and governs the world, and also of the natural law, which the Creator has written in our hearts, still there are not a few obstacles to prevent reason from making efficient and fruitful use of its natural ability. The truths that have to do with God and the relations between God and men, completely surpass the sensible order and demand self-surrender and self-abnegation in order to be put into practice and to influence practical life. Now the human intellect, in gaining the knowledge of such truths is hampered both by the activity of the senses and the imagination, and by evil passions arising from original sin. Hence men easily persuade themselves in such matters that what they do not wish to believe is false or at least doubtful.

It is for this reason that divine revelation must be considered morally necessary so that those religious and moral truths which are not of their nature beyond the reach of reason in the present condition of the human race, may be known by all

men readily with a firm certainty and
with freedom from all error. (2, 3)

Without faith, moral theology—indeed, all theology—would be merely an interesting subject to be
studied. It is the person of Christ who gives life to
the whole enterprise, and revelation gives us privileged access to life in Jesus Christ. It is no wonder
then that to be Christian we must immerse ourselves
in Scripture.

Our faith in Jesus Christ is essential to our being
Christians, while our intellect and reason enable us
to work out what our faith demands of us and how
we can grow in it. Theology itself is often described
as "faith seeking understanding," which brings these
two dimensions together.

John Paul II cogently displayed this dual emphasis on
Scripture and reason in his 1993 encyclical *Veritatis
Splendor* (The Splendour of Truth).[10] He began each
section with a scriptural quote that he then developed using a natural law–based approach, showing
how the two areas intertwine and complement each
other. At the beginning of the encyclical, he writes
that he set out to answer the question posed by the
rich young man: "Teacher, what good deed must I do
to have eternal life?" (Matthew 19:16) The encycli-

cal is a masterful response based on Gospel values and in light of church teaching through the ages.

5. Traditional moral theology: Objective dimensions

Since Roman Catholic moral theology is rooted in natural law, we can use our reason to make intelligent arguments about reality, based on our observing and analyzing situations. We make these observations about the nature of the person—that is, who we are as human beings—and what, as Aquinas said, is best for human flourishing.

Moral righteousness exists when the action under consideration enhances human flourishing. What constitutes enhancement is, of course, subject to debate. Natural law does not have all the answers. We must use reason to assess results or, perhaps, predict them in every situation that involves moral choices.

The virtue of prudence is necessary to inform reason, amounting to what Aquinas termed "right reason." He pointed out that the virtuous person is the one who will make the best judgments, since his or her mind will be the one that is most free of vice, bias or uninformed conscience. Reality determines the rightness or wrongness of a situation, which the prudent person is well placed to understand.

Pope John Paul II developed this idea in his encyclical *Veritatis Splendor*:

> The alleged conflict between freedom and nature also has repercussions on the interpretation of certain specific aspects of the natural law, especially its *universality and immutability*. "Where then are these rules written", Saint Augustine wondered, "except in the book of that light which is called truth? From thence every just law is transcribed and transferred to the heart of the man who works justice, not by wandering but by being, as it were, impressed upon it, just as the image from the ring passes over to the wax, and yet does not leave the ring."

> Precisely because of this "truth" *the natural law involves universality*. Inasmuch as it is inscribed in the rational nature of the person, it makes itself felt to all beings endowed with reason and living in history. In order to perfect himself in his specific order, the person must do good and avoid evil, be concerned for the transmission and preservation of life, refine and develop the riches of the material world,

cultivate social life, seek truth, practise good and contemplate beauty.

The separation which some have posited between the freedom of individuals and the nature which all have in common, as it emerges from certain philosophical theories which are highly influential in present-day culture, obscures the perception of the universality of the moral law on the part of reason. But inasmuch as the natural law expresses the dignity of the human person and lays the foundation for his fundamental rights and duties, it is universal in its precepts and its authority extends to all mankind. *This universality does not ignore the individuality of human beings*, nor is it opposed to the absolute uniqueness of each person. On the contrary, it embraces at its root each of the person's free acts, which are meant to bear witness to the universality of the true good. By submitting to the common law, our acts build up the true communion of persons and, by God's grace, practise charity, "which binds everything together in perfect harmony" (*Col* 3:14). When on the contrary they disregard the law, or

> even are merely ignorant of it, whether
> culpably or not, our acts damage the
> communion of persons, to the detriment
> of each. (51)

The Church bases its conclusions about the rightness and wrongness of behaviour on its effects on people. As such, natural law can be seen neither as completely permanent nor as unchangeable. When a specific situation becomes clearer or different circumstances begin to emerge, the Church must re-evaluate the behaviour in light of this new knowledge. Reason must always be applied in every situation, preventing ethical thinking from remaining static.

Natural law cannot be expressed fully at any point in history. For example, Aquinas based some of his conclusions on the science of female anatomy and physiology as it was known in his time. When we learned new facts about the female body, our idea of when life begins, or conception occurs, changed radically. Good ethics depends on good, accurate facts. Everyone knows that more is always being discovered about the way we operate as humans. This new knowledge has important applications for ethics and bioethics. Ethicists and bioethicists, as well as the whole teaching Church, must stay informed and always open to new possibilities.

6. Traditional moral theology: Subjective dimensions

We have just emphasized the importance of the objective dimension of Roman Catholic teaching and its universal applicability. This is a major claim, but one that can be proven to be accurate through logical thinking.

This objective system makes a universal theory of ethics possible. If there were no standards, what would we use to guide us in decision making? We would have to rely only on subjective thinking—what each person decides is best for herself or himself in a given situation. Earlier, we discussed relativism: how easy it would be to move to that state if there were no moral tenets that were true absolutely and on which reasonable people could agree. We can see that some activities do not enhance human flourishing and we have no hesitation in naming them as evils. At the same time, our individual thinking and reflecting is of great importance and is what makes us human.

Aquinas stressed the importance of reason, and our natural law–based approach to ethics rests squarely on that foundation.

In terms of being responsible, moral people, we must use our critical-thinking capacities. These are, of course, highly subjective, varying from person to person. Most of us realize that we are rather limited in our thinking in many areas of our lives; we depend on other people's superior capacities, while we contribute to society's development in other ways. We are interdependent, although some geniuses lead the way for us, blazing trails that the rest of us eventually follow.

This realization stops us from thinking that our own subjective thinking could always be accurate and complete. In most areas, we look to experts for advice and information. In our moral decision making, while we are ultimately responsible for those decisions and must make up our own minds, free of compulsion, it is dangerous to assume that our subjective reasoning is always correct in its conclusions. We know our limitations and we know we could be wrong. Untested subjective thinking could lead us astray, even when we are attempting to be good. At the same time, some points that are objectively true about a particular subject may not be universally true, such as the amount of pain one can tolerate. This is not to dismiss them as being merely subjective, however, as if they have no validity.

The teaching of the Church, on the other hand, has been formulated through the ages, whether at church councils, by popes or in documents issued by various congregations or pontifical councils. The teaching of theologians is also important; here we think especially of Doctors of the Church such as St. Augustine, St. Thomas Aquinas and St. Alphonsus, whose works, based on natural law, have been especially influential in Catholic thinking about morality.

7. Conscience

Linked with our capacity for reasoning is our reliance on our conscience, which innately calls us to assess our actions and to strive towards the good. Conscience is our reasoning capacity and our powers of observation and reflection at work. We are using conscience whenever we ask ourselves, what is the right thing to do in this situation? What should I do and what should I be like? It is through our actions that we shape ourselves. This, in turn, shapes our society, first though our family, then through our immediate relationships, and so on. Sometimes we forget that we are interconnected and that what we do as individuals very often has repercussions in society. Our moral actions have further reaching consequences than it may first appear.

The Roman Catholic Church holds conscience in high esteem. It tells us that, as long as we inform our conscience prayerfully and to the best of our ability (and that is extremely important), then any decision we make will be a good one, and even when what we decided turns out to be wrong, we have not sinned. A good conscience decision is the best we can do at some points in our lives, and the Church recognizes this fact.

At the same time, we must remember that sometimes our conscience decisions can turn out to be wrong. Nearly everyone experiences this at some point. This, too, is part of the human condition: we cannot be right all the time! We have to be careful, therefore, not to treat our own conscience decisions as infallible and accept that there is wisdom in church teaching, which inevitably surpasses our own.

Nevertheless, the guarantee of freedom of informed conscience is an important one for us as committed Catholics. As thinking people we know we are not sheep, slavishly following the rules of others. We have the responsibility to think things through for ourselves and to reflect on church teachings. Many people do not do this thoroughly enough. When we perform the tasks of conscience properly, we recognize the truth of the words of *Gaudium et Spes*: that it is here that we as individuals are closest to God.

> In the depths of his conscience, man detects a law which he does not impose upon himself, but which holds him to obedience. Always summoning him to love good and avoid evil, the voice of conscience when necessary speaks to his heart: do this, shun that. For man has in his heart a law written by God; to obey it is the very dignity of man; according to it he will be judged. Conscience is the most secret core and sanctuary of a man. There he is alone with God, Whose voice echoes in his depths. In a wonderful manner conscience reveals that law which is fulfilled by love of God and neighbor. In fidelity to conscience, Christians are joined with the rest of men in the search

for truth, and for the genuine solution to the numerous problems which arise in the life of individuals from social relationships. Hence the more right conscience holds sway, the more persons and groups turn aside from blind choice and strive to be guided by the objective norms of morality. Conscience frequently errs from invincible ignorance without losing its dignity. The same cannot be said for a man who cares but little for truth and goodness, or for a conscience which by degrees grows practically sightless as a result of habitual sin. (16)

8. Conversion

In his weekly general audience for February 21, 2007, which was Ash Wednesday, Pope Benedict XVI spoke of conversion in the context of Lent.

Lent is a renewed "catechumenate" … in which once again we approach our Baptism to rediscover and relive it in depth, to return to being truly Christian.

Lent is thus an opportunity to "become" Christian "anew", through a constant process of inner change and progress in the knowledge and love of Christ. Conversion is never once and for all but is a process, an interior journey through the whole of life.[11]

Conversion is the ongoing task of being fully Christian. No matter how good we are, there are always areas in ourselves that need to be changed. This realization comes upon us at various times. We only gradually become aware of our limitations and presumptions. It is easy for us to ignore our own shortcomings. It takes openness, and perhaps some outward intervention, to nudge us on to the next stage of our development.

If ever we wondered what grace is, it surely becomes apparent to us in those moments of moving closer to the truth of things. Those special moments, whether subtle or dramatic, lead us further towards our higher destiny as Christians. More than self-fulfillment, although including it, conversion makes us realize the power of God as our creator and patient guide on our path.

The call to conversion and the grace to answer that call are undeserved. Conversion happens, although we cannot make it happen. If we are open to that call, however, God's grace can break through our hardness of heart.

Part 2:

Reproductive technologies

1. The human person: Church teaching

When we see a new baby, we usually experience a sense of awe and wonder. Just about everyone's heart melts on seeing this example of the amazing power of life. The little one who grew in its mother's womb is now fully visible and making his or her presence felt. Is there any thinking and feeling person who does not stop to reflect on the meaning of existence when he or she meets a newborn? God gives us many chances to reflect, and the celebrations that take place on the occasion of a new birth are among the most joyous that occur. That is fitting: it reflects our gratitude and awe before the power of the creator who allows us to participate in this most wonderful aspect of all creation that we know—new human life.

It is unfortunate that, for many in our society, the prospect of new life is not greeted with joy. The attitude towards life is sometimes negative. Some lives are seen as undesirable. Our society has devised ways of disposing of them through abortion when the pregnancy is unwanted, when screening has identified a genetic or other medical problem, or even when the baby's sex is not what the parents desire.

But for those of us who are Christian, the idea that we are made in God's image should impel us to see how important every life is and how each one must be treated with respect. Catholic teaching rests on this foundation, respecting life unequivocally from conception until natural death.

2. Personhood: Theological and legal dimensions

Donum Vitae (The Gift of Life), an important church teaching from 1987, tells us that we are to be treated as persons from the moment of conception.[12] Personhood cannot be proved or disproved by philosophical argument; in fact, different jurisdictions have asserted that personhood begins at different times on the human developmental scale.

The law in the United Kingdom says we are not persons until we are born. Until we are persons by that definition we have no legal rights. That means that the woman (who can already be called a mother) is the only one during her pregnancy who has rights and, therefore, who may determine whether the baby should continue to exist or receive medical treatment. Many people find this argument irrational. The law in this and other countries has been open to challenge; in fact, mothers who have lost their unborn children as a result of a car accident have challenged it and have been awarded damages for their loss.

Catholic teaching emphasizes the personhood of the tiny organism that develops without interruption from the time of conception. Other views of personhood have to invent or decide upon other starting points, mainly to accommodate the intent to override any legal status the new life would otherwise acquire by virtue of existence.

Philosophers debate personhood, and laws may declare when personhood begins, but every woman who becomes pregnant knows that pregnancy of necessity means that another person (the father) is involved. Why else does pregnancy cause so much joy for some and so much anxiety for those who are not open to that new life? A societal denial about personhood enables us to allow abortion as a choice. This is not the case in every country, however, which further highlights the inadequacy and wrongness of most judicial and philosophical versions of personhood.

What we accept about persons from our biblical heritage applies to every person, including the embryo. From the Old Testament, we learn that our personhood flows from being made in God's image. In the New Testament, Paul tells us of the privilege we have in being part of the Body of Christ, as well as reminding us of the responsibilities we have to the members of the Body. These factors are important for Catholics to consider at every stage of life and are extremely relevant when it comes to technological ways of bringing human life into being.

3. The morality of in vitro fertilization

When couples are infertile, they often turn to reproductive technology. The process of in vitro fertilization allows a human embryo to be made in a petri dish, by fusing the parents' gametes (egg and sperm).

The Church teaches that this use of technology separates the unitive and procreative aspects of intercourse between husband and wife, and therefore is not allowed. With in vitro fertilization, new life depends on the impersonal acts of scientists and laboratory workers. The Church points out that it is completely against human dignity to bring a human child into the world this way, instead of through a personal, marital act of its own mother and father. Instead, Catholic teaching says that sexual intercourse between husband and wife is the most fitting way to conceive a child. *Gaudium et Spes* designates parents as "co-operators with the love of God the Creator," reflecting the importance of the parents' role (50).

Although conception through such a loving act does not happen for every couple, the Church emphasizes that this is what best fits our human dignity. A woman who becomes pregnant after being raped, or who has been coerced into becoming pregnant, does not have the opportunity to welcome her child in such a way. The respect due to the child and the child's dignity are the same as anyone else's, but we can see that the child's conception did not respect human dignity.

The Church, in *Donum Vitae*, states that respect for human dignity is similarly absent when a child is conceived through technological means such as in vitro fertilization:

> Every human being is always to be accepted as a gift and blessing of God. However, from the moral point of view

a truly responsible procreation vis-à-vis the unborn child must be the fruit of marriage.

For human procreation has specific characteristics by virtue of the personal dignity of the parents and of the children: the procreation of a new person, whereby the man and the woman collaborate with the power of the Creator, must be the fruit and the sign of the mutual self-giving of the spouses, of their love and of their fidelity. The fidelity of the spouses in the unity of marriage involves reciprocal respect of their right to become a father and a mother only through each other. The child has the right to be conceived, carried in the womb, brought into the world and brought up within marriage: it is through the secure and recognized relationship to his own parents that the child can discover his own identity and achieve his own proper human development. (1)

The teaching makes it clear that human life is to be brought into being only through intercourse between husband and wife, and that no third person is to be brought into the relationship through the donation of eggs or sperm, or through surrogacy. This teaching also recognizes the *child's* rights, which are usually neglected in questions of infertility.

4. Ethical concerns arising from in vitro fertilization

The process

Couples may seek in vitro fertilization when they are infertile or are having difficulties getting pregnant. Sometimes the woman does not ovulate regularly, which diminishes the chances of conception. Women usually produce one egg each month, but with in vitro fertilization, the woman's ovaries are hyper-stimulated by drugs to produce several. The eggs are extracted by a surgical procedure; suitable ones are fertilized by the husband's sperm in a petri dish. (In vitro means "in glass" in Latin.) The resulting embryos (if any) are then implanted, perhaps two or three at a time, in the woman's womb, in the hope that at least one will develop. The current success rate for in vitro fertilization is about 30 per cent, meaning that the woman, on average, needs several cycles of treatment to become pregnant.

Harm to the embryo

Any embryos that are not used are usually frozen and kept. They may or may not be used eventually to try to achieve implantation, but either way, according to *Donum Vitae*, their dignity is assaulted (I, 6). Questions of ownership of frozen embryos have arisen when, for example, the parents have both died in a plane crash. Who decides about the use or disposal of the embryos in these cases? Further concerns, such as the effects on the embryos of freezing over the long term and the preference for "fresh" eggs, add to the list of legal ownership and disposal problems that face society. While the law is concerned about ownership and consent, morally we should be concerned that these embryos are being viewed and treated as property rather than as people.

Embryos that are tested for genetic problems before implantation are most often rejected by the parents and discarded. Infertile couples may be desperate to have a child but are unlikely to implant a genetically defective embryo.

Harm to women

Retrieval of eggs after hyper-stimulation of the ovaries is a surgical procedure that carries the usual medical risks. Hyper-stimulation itself involves taking heavy doses of drugs, which may not be good for specific women. Full and informed consent is necessary, as in every other medical procedure.

Harm to the moral climate

Sometimes women cannot produce suitable eggs, so clinics obtain eggs from other women. When it is the man who is infertile, then sperm donors may similarly be sought. Catholic teaching makes it clear that bringing third parties into the marriage in this way is unacceptable because it separates the unitive and procreative dimensions of the sexual act of husband and wife.

It is not just the Catholic Church that finds the donation of gametes to be unacceptable and unethical. In vitro fertilization and its component parts raise numerous social and ethical concerns. For example, the resulting baby is not truly the child of the couple: only one of the spouses (or partners outside marriage) is the biological parent. This in itself raises further issues related, for example, to the child's genetic inheritance. People using in vitro fertilization must trust clinics, doctors and donors to properly screen the gametes being used. Screening of donors is not well regulated in many countries, if it is regulated at all.

Many donors want to remain anonymous, and many jurisdictions are moving to legislate to ensure their privacy. At the same time, children conceived as a result of donated gametes are entitled to know about their genetic inheritance, in order to make health care and other decisions as they mature. Some countries have a registry, similar to that for adoption, to inform people of the facts of their own biological history.

Women who become egg donors must be aware of the risks involved and the variation in practices from one country to another. In the United Kingdom, regulations state that eggs are not to be bought and sold in a commercial transaction.[13] There are some provisions for reasonable expenses, but not for the donation of either eggs or sperm. The situation is different in other countries. For example, in the United States, eggs and sperm may be bought and sold. These services are advertised in newspapers and on the Internet. Since women who donate eggs must undergo surgical procedures, it is unlikely that they will do so without compensation, and it is already clear that altruistic gestures in that regard are rare.[14] The United Kingdom does not allow compensation. Donation of human eggs has been so low that researchers are allowed to use animal eggs in some specific situations by the Human Fertilisation Embryology Authority (HFEA).[15]

Catholic teaching reminds us that most of these developments in reproductive technology radically affect people's attitude towards new human life. We are in a position to create life but also to reject it at the embryonic stage if it does not fit our expectations and demands. No longer are we co-operating with God; rather, we are operating in our own sphere, according to our own will, bringing all our human subjective biases and desires into play (*Donum Vitae*, II B 4 c).

Some couples choose surrogacy—that is, they hire a woman to have their embryo implanted in her womb, and she then brings the baby to term. Apart from the commercial nature of this type of transaction, the use of another party in this way is clearly in total contradiction to the covenant of marriage, and not only from a religious viewpoint. Even if one is not religious, the introduction of another woman to carry the couple's embryo to term – or, more commonly, to be impregnated with the paying husband's sperm to do so – surely changes the notion of "husband, wife and child." The child's biological inheritance will only partly be that of his or her "parents," and if both egg and sperm are donated, will not be the couple's biological child at all. Adoption would be a simpler option in some of these cases, with fewer moral dilemmas.

Clearly, infertility has become an industry with a life of its own, and it continues to generate moral problems. For example, some women freeze their eggs for their daughters' future use, should they be infertile. Other women donate or, more commonly, in other countries sell their eggs to women who require them. These situations raise some interesting societal concerns. For example, women who use their mothers' eggs will give birth to their own half sisters. This fact does not bother all ethicists, but even some secular ethicists are uncomfortable with the nature and outcome of these procedures. They wonder what kind of society we are developing and what we are doing to the structure of the family and family relationships.

The Catholic insistence on a child's being born from the intimate marital act of its mother and father is the only way to ensure that neither gametes nor embryos are viewed as property, commodified or treated in any way as the object of commercial transactions. Views that contradict Catholic teaching are shaping a moral climate that in many ways harms the dignity of the embryos and children concerned. By extension, this harms all of us who uphold the covenant of marriage and respect for human life.

One of the most obvious areas in which this harm is done is in the use of embryonic stem cells, taken from what are known as "no longer required" or, more commonly, "spare" embryos.[16] The Catholic Church is clear in its teaching that this use is morally evil, since experimentation results in the death of the embryo, a living human being at the earliest stages of existence. There are many other harms involved here, including the non-consent of the embryo, our using other humans for our perceived good, and the general non-recognition of the equal human dignity of these small human beings with that of the rest of society.

5. Stem cells: Embryonic and adult

What are stem cells?

Stem cells are cells found in various parts of the human body that are capable of regenerating tissues; thus, they are vital for repairing and renewing damaged tissue and organs. This process happens spontaneously in the body during the repair of minor damage, but not serious damage, for example, to heart muscles or valves. Experiments with animals and humans have shown that stem cells can be taken from other parts of the body and directed towards the damaged part; the stem cells have regenerated parts formerly not reparable.

Various sources of stem cells

Embryonic stem cells

Originally it was thought that human embryonic stem cells had the greatest potential to cure disease. That was partly because these cells are the newest and youngest cells available, but mainly because these are cells that have not yet "differentiated."

Up until about the fourteenth day of existence, before the embryo's cells organize themselves to become specific tissues and organs in the body, they seem to be capable of forming any organ or tissue: that is, they are "undifferentiated." After about fourteen days, the process of organization and differentiation begins. Cells are directed towards becoming specific parts of the body—organs, limbs, and so on. That is the reason why embryos that are created by in vitro fertilization must be implanted into the woman's uterus within fourteen days. Otherwise they must be frozen to preserve them for possible future use.

The fact that embryonic cells have not begun to differentiate before fourteen days is thought to be of the greatest importance, since this means that these cells should, theoretically at least, be of use in creating new tissue in any part of the body where repair is needed. The word used for this capacity is *totipotent*: these stem cells are thought capable of making new tissue or muscle for a damaged heart, kidney or liver, and so on.

Considerable research has been done with embryonic stem cells, so far mainly on animals, for obvious safety reasons. Several serious complications have arisen.

First, tumours have formed in many of the animals, despite some success in tissue regeneration. That makes the use of these treatments in humans impossible for the time being, since they are causing complications that would be as bad as, or even worse than, existing conditions.

Second, in nearly all the experiments, the animal's body has rejected the newly regenerated tissue. In humans, the body's rejection of imported embryonic stem cells would jeopardize any purported treatment. The patient would have to take immuno-suppressant drugs for the rest of his or her life in order to have the body accept the new tissue; these drugs have some serious side effects.

Third, but most important from the moral perspective, the embryo dies when it is used for experimentation. This means that even if the problems described above were solved, and even if the question of consent to the use of embryos were somehow resolved, we should still never use them.

Adult stem cells

Adult or somatic stem cells are distinct from embryonic stem cells and are obtainable from many sources
in the human body, including the following:

- specific parts of the body of the person to
  be treated, such as bone marrow, brain, liver,
  skeletal muscle and blood vessels;

- umbilical cords, which are recognized as a
  strong source of usable stem cells; and

- amniotic fluid during pregnancy; afterwards,
  a rich source is the placenta.

Most importantly, and not only from a Catholic viewpoint, obtaining these stem cells involves none of the
moral problems involved in extracting embryonic
stem cells, particularly the subsequent death of the
embryo. This means that there is an alternative to using embryonic stem cells for developing treatments
for serious illnesses.

It was originally thought that adult stem cells would
be of restricted use to repair or renew only the part
of the body from which they had been taken. This
made apparent sense, since in fact these cells had

differentiated and had continued to develop in those specific parts.

Nevertheless, researchers have continued their work on adult stem cells despite the general misgivings. After all, even if these cells turned out to be useful only in specific areas, that in itself would be useful. Research and experimentation, however, have revealed a much broader spectrum of use for adult stem cells than expected. According to the American National Institutes of Health,

> Adult stem cells, such as blood-forming stem cells in bone marrow (called hematopoietic stem cells, or HSCs), are currently the only type of stem cell commonly used to treat human diseases. Doctors have been transferring HSCs in bone marrow transplants for over 40 years. More advanced techniques of collecting, or "harvesting," HSCs are now used in order to treat leukemia, lymphoma and several inherited blood disorders.

> The clinical potential of adult stem cells has also been demonstrated in the treatment of other human diseases, including diabetes and advanced kidney cancer. However, these newer uses have

involved studies with a very limited
number of patients.[17]

The use of adult stem cells is more promising for
humans in other ways, especially since they do not
carry the same risk of rejection as embryonic stem
cells. The use of one's own cells means that immuno-
suppressant drugs are not necessary.

Scientists recently discovered how to insert genes
into adult skin cells to reprogram them to behave
like embryonic stem cells. If treatment for diseases
do result from this method, then many ethical issues
will be resolved if stem cells from human embryos
will no longer be needed.[18]

6. Stem cell experimentation and morality

Catholic teaching and the use of human embryonic stem cells

As mentioned earlier, not all embryos created
through in vitro fertilization are implanted. The use
of phrases such as *no longer required* and *spare* to
describe unwanted embryos shows how easy it is to
downplay the fact of the humanity of every embryo,

made in God's image. We never consider ourselves to be spare and should never use that term for others, even at the embryonic stage. From the Catholic perspective, each embryo must be treated as a person. That means an embryo may never be used in order to achieve an unrelated goal or as a way to meet a perceived need. Regardless of the types of cure that are predicted as result of embryonic stem cell experimentation, embryos must not be used in this way. Catholic teaching is clear that this experimentation is never morally permissible.

Further moral consequences of the use of embryonic stem cells

Most unused embryos stay frozen until the parents want to implant them or perhaps until something happens to reduce their utility, in which case the parents discard them. There have been cases of embryos defrosting because of power failures, resulting in their subsequent loss.

The question of legal ownership of stored embryos has arisen on numerous occasions. For example, in cases of divorce, to which partner do they belong? Frozen embryos swiftly become seen as property, to be transferred or given away by their parents in a contract or will.

There is currently the possibility of embryo adoption, by which couples decide that the wife will have someone else's embryo implanted in her womb, to save it from the frozen state, and give birth to it. The Catholic Church has not yet made a specific pronouncement on the morality of this practice.

Catholic teaching and the use of adult stem cells

Obtaining adult stem cells involves none of the moral problems involved in extracting embryonic stem cells. It is clear that Catholic teaching can and does support medical advances using adult stem cells, since the Church, too, hopes that cures for many serious medical problems will be found through this new type of treatment.

7. The principle of double effect

People follow the principle of double effect in many situations, often to do with bioethics, when they have to decide whether to do something that will have two effects at the same time: one good, the other evil. We know that we are never allowed to cause moral evil directly. (Choosing moral evil to attain a proposed good is never acceptable.) But sometimes an action will have as its direct intention an effect that is good, while at the same time causing some foreseen harm. The principle of double effect says that it is permissible to act when four conditions are met simultaneously:

- the action itself is good, or morally neutral;

- the good effect does not come through the evil effect;

- the evil effect is not directly intended; and

- there is a proportionate reason to allow the evil effect.

When these four conditions are met, then we are morally allowed to go ahead with the action. We must remember, however, that we are talking about a principle here; it can be useful to help us structure our moral thinking, but we must be aware of its limitations.

8. Co-operation in evil

Christians are asked to seek the good always and shun evil. However, good is sometimes inextricably connected with evil.

When another person who is the principal agent chooses the evil, is it ever legitimate to be involved in his or her action in any way? The traditional principle of co-operation in evil helps us here.

The main division in co-operation is between formal and material co-operation. Formal co-operation involves our intentionally supporting the evil choice of the principal agent. When a surgical theatre nurse who favours choice in the matter of abortion helps a surgeon perform it, she co-operates formally. Material co-operation means we are involved in the action of the principal agent, but without approving or wishing the intended end. The reason why we are co-operating at all must be to prevent greater harm if we did not co-operate. An example of legitimate material co-operation is opening the vault of a bank for robbers with guns. The material co-operation may be immediate (part of the action itself) or mediate (not part of the actual action, but proximate [near it] or remote [far from it]).

Immediate material co-operation demands a more serious reason than does mediate co-operation. Proximate co-operation requires a more urgent reason than does remote co-operation.

An associated idea is complicity. Complicity does not involve our aiding the achievement of the principal agent's purpose. Rather, it consists of our benefiting from his or her actions and so showing approval of what took place, and perhaps smoothing the path for further evil actions. An example is benefiting from the use of embryonic stem cell experimentation, even as one denounces the destruction of embryos.

If researchers in a Catholic hospital conduct embryonic stem cell experimentation on stem cell lines obtained from another source, then they are being complicit in the destruction of the embryos which gave rise to the stem cell lines. Catholic teaching clearly condemns such destruction, and the researchers co-operate in evil if they obtain new stem cell lines when older ones become unstable. While they do not destroy the embryos, they do nothing to prevent this evil, and at the same time are benefiting from using the resulting stem cell lines for research.

Part 3:

End-of-life issues

1. The dignity of the dying

Personhood at the end of life

As discussed in Part 2, Roman Catholic teaching is concerned about the life of the person from the time of conception until natural death. Every person is made in God's image, and we must treat each person accordingly. Not surprisingly, this gives us a high standard against which to judge what we can and cannot do with and to our own lives and bodies and those of all others. The Second Vatican Council said in *Gaudium et Spes*, "The human being alone is a person: he has the dignity of a subject and is of value in himself" (24). There are many teachings in this area, all aimed at ensuring that our dignity and value as persons are always respected, including at the end of life, even amid some difficult situations.

Being part of the Body of Christ further demands that we make sure that each person's dignity is maintained and respected throughout life, taking special care to do so during vulnerable times—at birth, in sickness and in dying.

This is second nature to most of us. We learn this approach by being part of loving and loyal families and also through our relationships with our close friends. We instinctively look out for their well-being in these situations. The Christian tries to ensure that this type of practical love is extended to everyone. It is the hallmark of Christian faith to love one another, and caring for each other at vulnerable times is part of that love.

From the legal point of view, the concept of personhood is framed these days in terms of the autonomy of the person. There are some advantages to this approach for the person. It means that the person is the one who consents to proposed medical treatment or, indeed, rejects it. Assuming the person is mentally competent, decision making rests with him or her, and family members or physicians may not insist on giving or withdrawing treatment. The person's rights are safeguarded within legal limits, and nothing should be done without his or her consent.

Care of the dying

The Christian approach to taking care of the sick and dying has long been exemplified by the many religious women and men who founded the first hospitals in most countries in the West and whose successors still work in health care in many cases. Care of the body has always been done in conjunction with care of the soul, mirroring the non-dualistic approach to the human person of Catholic teaching. John Paul II noted, "Every human person, in his unrepeatable uniqueness, is made up not only of spirit but also of a body, so that in the body and through it the person is reached in his concrete reality."[19]

At the Eucharist, parish communities pray for the sick, the dying and those who have died. This important part of our regular liturgical celebrations shows how the Christian community keeps its members in mind, both the living and those who have reached eternal life.

The Church reminds us that when people reach the last stages of life they have "… a right to die in total serenity, with human and Christian dignity."[20]

Christians see dying as the most important part of life, the final step in "going to the house of the Father," as John Paul II put it at the time of his impending death. The dying person deserves to have all assistance possible to ensure that these last days are as fruitful as possible.

This may involve help from outside the family, from pastors, health care professionals, social workers and eventually palliative care specialists. No one should feel abandoned at this special time. John Paul II emphasized that the most important service we can render a dying person is "loving presence."[21]

The Pontifical Council for Health Pastoral Care, in its *Charter for Health Care Workers*, reminds health care professionals (and everyone else) that this loving presence is even more important to patients than is professional expertise, inasmuch as "… it gives confidence and hope to the patient and makes him reconciled to death."[22]

Truth telling and the dying person

We expect that our family and friends will tell us the truth when we are living out our ordinary relationships. We hope that other groups and institutions will do the same. We try to live as if that were the case, until facts tell differently. It is part of human dignity to be told the truth regarding matters that concern us as individuals, including our own physical health and condition. Information about a person's health should not be withheld when the person needs that information to make end-of-life decisions.

There are many reasons for this. First, there is the legal reason, based on the person's autonomy and right to know about his or her condition.

Second, there is a Christian duty to inform people about factors that are distressing to them, so that they might gradually face reality, come to terms with the truth of their condition and put their affairs in order, while still maintaining their human dignity.

Third, and extremely important for Christians, is that knowing the truth of their situation allows those who are dying to reconcile themselves to that fact and to reconcile with God and with their family and friends.

The Pontifical Council for Health Pastoral Care puts it well when it says, "Death is too essential a moment for its prospect to be avoided."[23] Of course, that does not mean that truth telling should be done ruthlessly, in an inhumane way; rather, it must be done in love, with all due respect for the person's dignity, condition and current state. Those who give patients factual information of a terminal illness have a difficult task, since they must communicate concern and compassion for the person as well as the medical details of the situation.

2. Patients' rights

Just as health care workers have duties and responsibilities towards patients, and rights as workers,
patients have their own rights and responsibilities.
These are the mirror image of society's responsibilities towards them. Patient autonomy is strongly
emphasized currently, but patients are also owed
justice, care and concern. Some hospitals have charters of patients' rights; some countries have similar
charters, protecting patients against possible abuses
during their stay in hospital and other facilities. The
reality of abuse of vulnerable people is well known,
as evidenced by documented cases of abuse of senior
citizens, for example. The purpose of these charters
is to help make people aware of their rights when
they are patients. The charters let them know how
they or their families can address situations that are
unjust, that cause physical harm or damage people's
dignity and self-esteem.

Patients also have responsibilities, including the
provision of an accurate medical history, as well as
pertinent information about family illnesses. They
must seek clarification if they do not understand
their treatment policy, and have the duty to co-operate with that plan once they have given their consent

to its initiation. They must keep their hospital appointments, and should try to maintain a healthy lifestyle.

3. Withdrawal of treatment

Decision making

Most of us recognize that modern science and technology have made many more medical interventions possible than previously. Sometimes knowing when and when not to use or take advantage of these technologies can be difficult. We have to use every available resource when making decisions about our use of these technologies, including Catholic teaching, relevant medical facts and our own experience of making sound, prudent judgments.

Sometimes these technological aids are obviously beneficial and so present no moral problems. When it becomes clear that there is no longer any benefit from such technology, a decision may have to be made about stopping a treatment.

Ordinary/extraordinary or proportionate/ disproportionate treatment

Some long-standing principles in Catholic teaching help us make decisions about treatments. First, the Church tells us that we are always bound to use certain life-sustaining measures. These are the basic necessities of life, including food, water, air, rest and warmth. John Paul II added to this idea of the importance of our giving and accepting "basic care." He stated in 2004 that the artificial provision of food and water counts as basic care for patients in a persistent vegetative state.[24] He explained,

> I should like particularly to underline how the administration of water and food, even when provided by artificial means, always represents a *natural means* of preserving life, not a *medical act*. Its use, furthermore, should be considered, in principle, *ordinary* and *proportionate*, and as such morally obligatory, insofar as and until it is seen to have attained its proper finality, which in the present case consists in providing nourishment to the patient and alleviation of his suffering. (4)

This leads us into a discussion of the difference between ordinary and extraordinary means of preserving life. Ordinary means are those without undue burden, that are effective and that are morally required. Extraordinary means cause undue burden, are ineffective and are not morally required. Doctors use these terms differently, however. For medical people, *ordinary* means are those commonly in use. *Extraordinary* means are experimental, pose a danger or are very expensive. In ethics, even means that are ordinary in a medical sense can be extraordinary because of the particular circumstances of the patient. The church document *Declaration on Euthanasia* uses the terms *proportionate* and *disproportionate* to better express the ethical aspects of end-of-life situations.[25] Part 4 will look more closely at the issue of euthanasia.

Burdensomeness

Some treatments are invasive or have serious side effects that cause certain individuals to refuse them. While some people are willing to undergo a long course of chemotherapy or to live permanently on a ventilator, others may find it an unacceptable burden. The Church tells us that people may make their decisions about such treatments based on their subjective response. They are not obliged to undergo treatment that causes them disproportionate physical or psychological distress.

Ineffective treatment

Another reason for discontinuing treatment is when it is no longer effective—that is, when it can no longer cure the patient. Palliative care is a different matter, since any treatment is given not to cure but to relieve symptoms and pain, with the intention of providing as much comfort as possible. In all other cases, it makes sense that we would not continue using something that does not work, and we would make this decision to stop a treatment when faced with the factual evidence. To continue using a means that does not achieve an end would be clearly disproportionate.

Pope John Paul II's statement on artificial nutrition and hydration

The Pope's 2004 statement about the artificial provision of food and water counting as basic care reversed a common opinion among theologians that artificial nutrition and hydration was a technology that should be judged as an ordinary or extraordinary means of preserving life, depending on circumstances. Moral theologians and physicians are exploring the implications of his teaching. It does not extend to situations other than when a person is in a persistent vegetative state, although this is perhaps a little unclear at the moment. Some people had regarded artificial nutrition and hydration of a patient in a persistent vegetative state as ineffective, since it does not cure the underlying illness—nothing can—nor does it contribute anything that the patient can experience as personal benefit. The patient has no capacity whatsoever for self-awareness or for interaction with others. Furthermore, he or she has no potential for regaining either of these abilities.

This is not a "quality of life" judgment that this patient's life is so radically impaired that he or she is better off dead. This patient is a person, and we are incapable of making such a judgment, which literally belongs to God alone. Rather, it is a realistic appraisal of whether there are reasons for continuing to provide artificial nutrition and hydration. The patient does not experience anything, because the upper and lower brain are destroyed; only the brain stem remains operative. Pope John Paul II's statement is important because it seems to settle a long-disputed matter. Wider discussion by moral theologians and physicians is ensuing to interpret its wisdom in light of traditional church teaching in this area.

Pain and suffering

Many end-of-life illnesses involve pain and suffering. Much progress has been made in the treatment of physical pain. Pain relief specialists tell us that in nearly all cases, pain can be alleviated. The Catholic Church tells us that relief of pain is a good thing and that we may take advantage of pain medication when necessary.[26]

Some severe illnesses require strong drugs. For these to be effective in certain cases, amounts may cause patients to lapse into unconsciousness. There is the possibility that the medication may even hasten death by a few days. When opioid medication became available in the 1940s, Pope Pius XII used the principle of double effect to explain that Roman Catholics may use them in serious cases to reduce pain, even if they do have the side effect of shortening life.[27] *Terminal sedation* is the medical term used for intentionally giving sedatives during a terminal illness to cause unconsciousness, even permanent unconsciousness. Pius's teaching reassures us that, since we are not intending death, and are intending relief of pain and suffering, then it is morally permissible to make use of sedatives in this way. This is consoling for many of us who may be apprehensive as to how we will handle the possibility of extreme pain.

Some people have started to use *terminal sedation* to mean giving patients at the end of life higher levels of sedation than would simply relieve pain, with the intention of bringing about death. We would call that, more straightforwardly, euthanasia. There is clearly a world of difference between causing death and relieving pain. Some have suggested *palliative sedation* as a better term for the latter, but in fact it is the intention of the person administering the drugs that determines what is really happening.

Other forms of suffering

Although sometimes used to explain the experience of physical pain, suffering also deals with the emotional and psychological aspects of the anguish we experience during severe life-threatening or terminal illnesses.

Some people talk of stages of dying, the process a person goes through on hearing news of his or her impending death, and the subsequent emotional and psychological responses to that news, as well as to the physical implications of the illness.[28]

Pope Pius XII was very pastoral in his approach to people with terminal illnesses. He reminded us that our spiritual duties at this time in life are of the utmost importance and must be addressed. This makes sense to us when we stop to reflect on the meaning and experience of death. Since we believe in death *and* resurrection, going to meet God is the most important thing we will ever do. Accordingly, we are encouraged to right our relationship with God through the sacraments of reconciliation, anointing of the sick and the Eucharist, and right our relationships with our loved ones, as far as humanly possible.

Part 4:

Catholic teaching on living life until the end

Life is God's gift to each person. It cannot be the object of human domination, either by the person who decides to intentionally reject his or her own life or by anyone who would kill a person or provide the means of suicide. We are made in God's image and are children of God. Our inherent dignity, then, demands the inviolability of every life.

Death comes to all of us, but we do not bring it upon ourselves; preferring nothingness to continuing life is a sign that we have lost hope in God and in other people. So often people are depressed at the end of life and see their life as a burden. It is up to us as members of the Body of Christ to do all that is humanly possible, including using medication, to make life bearable, if not joyful. The Church's *Declaration on Euthanasia* emphasizes this point, saying, "but believers see in life something greater, namely, a gift of God's love, which they are called upon to preserve and make fruitful."[29]

The religious rejection of euthanasia and physician-assisted suicide is powerful when we acknowledge God's dominion over us humans and all the earth. We need, though, to put forward other arguments that make sense to those who have no religious faith or do not believe in God.

1. Definitions

What is euthanasia? Pope John Paul II told us clearly in *Evangelium Vitae* (The Gospel of Life)[30]: "Euthanasia in the strict sense is understood to be an action or omission which of itself and by intention causes death, with the purpose of eliminating all suffering" (65).

The Catholic Church raises some arguments against the practice of euthanasia that have broad appeal. First, there is the ancient admonition to doctors: "Do no harm!" The mission of physicians is to cure people, to help them through their illnesses and to promote human health and vitality. It is dangerous to have members of the same profession responsible for euthanizing patients, deliberately taking life. They may do it as a sign of compassion, but many point out that it has to be clear what compassion means. There is nothing inherent in the accepted meaning of *compassion* that implies ending life to eliminate suffering. Rather, it has always been taken to mean that we share the person's suffering with him or her and do our best to ameliorate the situation. We noted earlier that Catholic teaching is clear that extreme suffering is treatable by a high level of medication, and that this is morally acceptable.

Second, there is a risk that the doctor-patient relationship will be damaged by this kind of expansion of the physician's role. Patients may not trust someone who has the potential to end their lives without their consent in some situations. The doctor-patient relationship is a privileged one, and requires high levels of trust for it to function properly. Patients want to know that doctors have their best interests at heart and that their doctors are being as truthful and honest as possible with them.

Third, physicians will find legalization or acceptance of euthanasia to be another challenge to their individual conscience and will have to find ways to protect their own rights. Catholic hospitals will also have to continue their opposition to these practices, which will add one more item to the list of practices in which Catholic hospitals may not and will not engage.

Fourth, allowing the deliberate taking of life will contribute to what Pope John Paul II, in his 1995 encyclical *Evangelium Vitae* (The Gospel of Life), called "the culture of death" (12). By that he meant that the accumulation of practices, such as euthanasia and abortion, that look to death to solve health and social problems leads the general population to think that the taking of life is acceptable for various reasons. We need to be clear about the difference between law and morality, and to know what our Church says about this difference. In *Evangelium Vitae*, Pope John Paul II noted that in some countries, the legalization of procedures such as abortion means that "choices once unanimously considered criminal and rejected by the common moral sense are gradually becoming socially acceptable" (31). The fact that law and society pronounce some actions legal does not detract from their inherent immorality.

Types of euthanasia

Both the *Declaration on Euthanasia* and *The Gospel of Life* dispense with the notion of active and passive euthanasia. These documents simply say that the deliberate killing of a person by act or omission in order to eliminate suffering is euthanasia.[31]

2. The Dutch experience

The moral landscape surrounding euthanasia changed radically in 2002 when the Netherlands declared that physicians would not be criminally charged in circumstances of euthanasia and physician-assisted suicide, as long as they followed a certain protocol. This protocol demands that the person requesting euthanasia be of sound mind and has requested euthanasia voluntarily, be suffering from a terminal illness, be suffering unbearable pain and be at least 16 years of age at the time of asking.

Although these criteria seem clear, experience has shown that they have been more or less ignored. For example, although consent is required, in many instances euthanasia has been performed on non-consenting people. This means that family members and doctors have decided, out of "compassion," to kill people who have not requested it. The dangers this practice poses and the possibilities of abuse are apparent.

Euthanasia has also been performed on people with an illness that will progressively worsen, in anticipation of the terminal phase and to avoid enduring that stage. Moreover, the fact that the person will have to endure such pain has become enough to ask for euthanasia, again to avoid having to deal with the pain. Finally, children younger than 16 with a serious illness or disability have been euthanized at the request of their parents. A protocol was devised at

Groningen, the Netherlands, in 2004 (and was later implemented), stating that severely handicapped newborns are not to be treated but rather should be euthanized, if the parents give consent.

Some claim that legalization prevents abuses of euthanasia and physician-assisted suicide, but it is clear that the initial requirements and safeguards have not been rigorously applied in the Netherlands. The further practices just described are not regarded as illegal there, if certain requirements are met: these are mainly to do with making sure the process is transparent and that a second medical practitioner approves the killing. The point is that such further practices and abuses are inevitable, and were, in fact, predicted when the Netherlands moved towards a permissive approach to killing in certain circumstances.

Other countries are looking at the Dutch developments. In fact, the Canadian Minister of Justice introduced a Bill in the House of Commons in February 2005 proposing that euthanasia and physician-assisted suicide be allowed in that country. The Bill fell when the government changed, but it serves as a strong indication that Canada could move towards legalizing these two practices.

3. Suffering and palliative care

One of the most important reasons for the possible acceptance of euthanasia is fear of suffering. Some illnesses do carry the prospect of great suffering, and this is clearly a worry for most people, as well as for their family and caregivers. The Catholic Church takes a realistic approach here. Suffering is highly individual and subjective. Only the person involved knows the level to which he or she can cope.

As we saw earlier in Part 3, Pope Pius XII said that we may control pain and suffering even to the extent of lapsing into unconsciousness, as long as we had completed our spiritual duties. He was clear that we may choose to endure the suffering for spiritual reasons but that nothing heroic is demanded of us. The decision about what to do in these situations is ours to make. We may take strong medication to alleviate pain; the one thing we must never do is actively cause death.

When we reach the point that no medical intervention will cure us, we must face the fact that our illness is terminal and that in the end stages we may need considerable fortitude. The role of palliative care becomes extremely important in trying to ensure that our physical suffering is reduced as far as possible. Even more important, palliative care at its best reassures us that we will not have to face the last stages of life alone.

The universal availability of palliative care is something that we cannot take for granted. The political will to make universal palliative care a reality needs to be more forceful, strengthening the budget allocated for actual care and for training in palliative medicine in medical schools. In addition, not enough physicians have had adequate training in this field, which also needs to be recognized and addressed.

From the moral point of view, good palliative care is essential to the care of the sick and dying, and is one of the best ways to be compassionate at the end of life. If people think that they will have to suffer because of the lack of palliative medicine, then the case for legalizing euthanasia is strengthened. Some have suggested that the cost of palliative care will stretch our limited medical resources. They argue that euthanasia and physician-assisted suicide are far less costly than palliative care, and may be attractive from that point of view alone.

If we see palliative care as a good and necessary part of end-of-life care, we must be more aware of political realities and movements to provide it and support their efforts. We must also be more aware of movements to promote euthanasia and physician-assisted suicide as solutions to suffering and end-of-life care, and voice our concerns.

4. The Christian approach to death

As Christians, we know that death is a mystery, an unknown quantity. We do not see death as an end in itself but as a transition to fullness of life in God through the power of Christ's resurrection. Death is anything but pointless in this view; it is the inevitable end of the earthly part of our existence, but leads to what we hope and believe in—eternal life with God. While we must endure human pain at the end of life in the same way as every other human person, our belief gives a different character to the end of life. We see it in the words of Pope John Paul II, in his inspirational *Letter to the Elderly*, as going "from life to life!" (17).[32] In this letter he vividly portrays how he continued to enjoy life, despite the inevitable limitations of old age, saying, "It is wonderful to be able to give oneself to the very end for the sake of the Kingdom of God!" (17)

He adds,

> And so I often find myself saying, with no trace of melancholy, a prayer recited by priests after the celebration of the Eucharist: *In hora mortis meae voca me, et iube me venire ad te*—at the hour of my death, call me and bid me come to you. This is the prayer of Christian hope, which in no way detracts from the joy of the present, while entrusting the future to God's gracious and loving care. (17)

We, too, can take heart from his words as we reflect on death and realize that the hope so joyfully expressed in his message is possible for each of us when the time comes.

Appendix:
Advance directives
for health care

Many interventions are possible when something goes seriously wrong with a person's health. Decisions regarding health care sometimes have to be made when the patient is incapable of making them. With advance directives, we can outline what we would like to happen in the event of our becoming incapacitated. We can spell out the circumstances in which we would want to have certain treatments and reject others. In this way, we are able to control what happens, at least to some degree. We will not be at the mercy of other people, nor be leaving people in the difficult position of having to work out what we would or would not want. The media has made us aware of many distressing situations in which people are faced with real moral dilemmas of this type.

By preparing advance directives, many people have prepared for the possibility of that sort of problem arising for them.

Living wills

We can write out our wishes as fully as possible and try to anticipate every conceivable scenario. If we do this, and we sign it and date the document, then it is legally valid. We should be sure to leave it somewhere accessible, or give it to our doctor or a trusted family member so that, in the event of our not being able to speak for ourselves, it will be followed. Medical personnel will be obliged to carry out our wishes, as far as possible.

These documents are sometimes called "living wills." They have lost popularity of late, mainly because it is difficult to be clear about one's wishes ahead of time. If we are too specific, we may end up having treatment we do not want. Conversely, those acting on our behalf might be prevented from taking some action that could be life-saving. Living wills may be useful, but at times they do not work to the person's advantage.

Powers of attorney

Under the Mental Capacity Act, 2005, provision has been made in the United Kingdom for powers of attorney in cases where people are unable to speak on their own behalf. For health care matters, the relevant document is called a Lasting Power of Attorney. A comprehensive discussion of these important matters from a Catholic point of view of end-of-life decisions is found in a document issued by the Catholic Bishops Conference of England and Wales.[33]

We can be as specific as we wish about what we would or would not want done in certain situations; we can leave the judgment entirely to the person named. There are many possibilities with this latter type of document. It is now commonly thought to be better than the earlier, more detailed type of advance directive. That is partly because it is more open-ended, since it is difficult to know in advance what type of situation we are likely to be in.

When naming our attorney, it is important to remember that we are giving considerable power to someone to make good judgments in our best interests. The person must promise to follow our wishes as far as possible. It is clear that in naming our attorney, we should choose someone whom we can trust and who can make good judgments, in accordance with sound morality. Most likely it will be a family member, but we must still be prudent in whom we choose.

We have to tell the person that we have named him or her, and the person has to be willing to accept the responsibility. There are no surprises here: we must share the information about what we would like to have done and discuss our wishes.

There can be more than one person named. In that case, it would make sense that it be more than two, so that a voting majority is possible should a decision not be unanimous.

Power of attorney documents, like any living will, should be kept somewhere safe, given to the person we have chosen to act on our behalf, our physician, lawyer or long-term care administrator, or other appropriate people. A very important factor about any advance directive is that it be available when it is needed. A power of attorney document must be dated and signed to be legally effective. Power of attorney forms are readily obtainable from provincial government offices and on the Internet.

Notes

1   Pope John Paul II. *Man and Woman He Created Them: A Theology of the Body*. Boston: Pauline Books and Media (2006) I, section 3, 156.

2   International Theological Commission. *Communion and Stewardship: Human Persons Created in the Image of God*. (July 2004) IV, section 9, 254–286.

3   *Communion and Stewardship*, section 26.

4   *Communion and Stewardship*, section 25.

5   Richard M. Gula. *Reason Informed by Faith*. Mahwah, NJ: Paulist Press, 1989, 166.

6   Quoted in Gula, *Reason Informed by Faith*, 169–171.

7   Pope Paul VI. *Optatam Totius* (On Priestly Formation), 1965, 16. http://www.vatican.va/archive/hist_councils/ ii_vatican_council/documents/vat-ii_decree_ 19651028_optatam-totius_en.html. Accessed January 23, 2008.

8   Pope Paul VI. *Gaudium et Spes*, 1965. http://www. vatican.va/archive/hist_councils/ii_vatican_council/

documents/vat-ii_cons_19651207_gaudium-et-spes_
en.html. Accessed January 23, 2008.

9   Pope Pius XII. *Humani Generis* 1950. http://www.
    vatican.va/holy_father/pius_xii/encyclicals/documents/
    hf_p-xii_enc_12081950_humani-generis_en.html.
    Accessed January 23, 2008.

10 Pope John Paul II. *Veritatis Splendor*, 1993. http://
    www.vatican.va/holy_father/john_paul_ii/encyclicals/
    documents/hf_jp-ii_enc_06081993_veritatis-splendor_
    en.html. Accessed January 23, 2008.

11 Pope Benedict XVI. General Audience, February 21,
    2007. http://www.vatican.va/holy_father/benedict_
    xvi/audiences/2007/documents/hf_ben-xvi_aud_
    20070221_en.html. Accessed January 23, 2008.

12 Congregation for the Doctrine of the Faith. *Donum
    Vitae*, 1987. http://www.vatican.va/roman_curia/
    congregations/cfaith/documents/rc_con_cfaith_doc_
    19870222_respect-for-human-life_en.html. Accessed
    January 23, 2008.

13 These matters were originally regulated in the UK by
    the Human Fertilisation and Embryology Act 1990, and
    now by the Human Fertilisation and Embryology Act
    2008.

14 BBC News. "Stem Cell Finding Offers IVF Hope."
    http://news.bbc.co.uk/1/hi/health/4104680.stm.
    Accessed February 6, 2008. "Pay IVF Donors $10,000:
    expert." http://www.testtubebabyclinic.com/html/
    related/articles/2002h.asp. Accessed February 6, 2008.

15 The use of animal eggs, producing hybrid or inter-
    species embryos for experimentation purposes; is now
    regulated by the Human Fertilisation and Embryology
    Act 2008.

16 Updated Guidelines for Human Pluripotent Cell
    Research, Candian Institutes of Health Research
    (CIHR) (2006) Section 8 1.1, http://www.cihr-irsc.
    gc.ca/e/34460.html.

17 NIH Stem Cell Information website: http://stemcells.
    nih.gov/info/faqs.asp#content. Accessed June 24,
    2007.

18 Moira McQueen, "What's Happening in the World of
    Stem Cells and Cloning?" *Bioethics Update*. Volume
    7, No. 3, December 2007, http://www.ccbi-utoronto.
    ca/documents/bioethic_update/2007_Stem%20Cell
    s%20&%20Cloning.pdf" http://www.ccbi-utoronto.
    ca/documents/bioethic_update/2007_Stem%20Cells%
    20&%20Cloning.pdf Accessed October 10 2008.

19 Pope John Paul II. *To the Participants at the 35th
    General Assembly of the World Medical Association.*
    AAS 76 (1984), 393.

20 Congregation for the Doctrine of the Faith, *Declaration
    on Euthanasia*, 1980. http://www.vatican.va/roman_
    curia/congregations/cfaith/documents/rc_con_cfaith_
    doc_19800505_euthanasia_en.html. Accessed January
    23, 2008.

24 Pope John Paul II. Address to the Participants in the International Congress on "Life-Sustaining Treatments and Vegetative State: Scientific Advances and Ethical Dilemmas," March 20, 2004. http://www.vatican.va/holy_father/john_paul_ii/ speeches/2004/march/documents/hf_jp-ii_spe_ 20040320_congress-fiamc_en.html. Accessed January 23, 2008.

25 Sacred Congregation for the Doctrine of the Faith. *Declaration on Euthanasia*, 1980. IV. http://www. vatican.va/roman_curia/congregations/cfaith/ documents/rc_con_cfaith_doc_19800505_ euthanasia_en.html. Accessed January 23, 2008.

26 Pope Pius XII. Address to an International Congress of Anaesthesiologists. AAS 49 (1957).

27 Ibid.

28 According to Elisabeth Kübler-Ross's groundbreaking research, the five stages are denial, anger, bargaining, depression and acceptance. Elisabeth Kübler-Ross, *On Death and Dying* (New York: Simon and Schuster, 1997).

29 *Declaration on Euthanasia*, I.

30 Pope John Paul II. *Evangelium Vitae*, 1995. http://www.vatican.va/holy_father/john_paul_ii/ encyclicals/documents/hf_jp-ii_enc_25031995_ evangelium-vitae_en.html. Accessed January 23, 2008.

31 Congregation for the Doctrine of the Faith,
    Declaration on Euthanasia. "By euthanasia is
    understood an action or an omission which of
    itself or by intention causes death, in order that all
    suffering may in this way be eliminated." (Part II)
    Pope John Paul II, *Evangelium Vitae*, 1993. For a
    correct moral judgment on euthanasia, in the first
    place a clear definition is required. Euthanasia in the
    strict sense is understood to be an action or omission
    which of itself and by intention causes death, with
    the purpose of eliminating all suffering. Euthanasia's
    terms of reference, therefore, are to be found in the
    intention of the will and in the methods used." (65)

32 Pope John Paul II. *Letter to the Elderly*, 1999.
    http://www.vatican.va/holy_father/john_paul_ii/
    letters/documents/hf_jp-ii_let_01101999_elderly_
    en.html. Accessed January 23, 2008.

33 The Catholic Bishops conference of England and
    Wales. *The Mental Capacity Act and 'Living Wills':
    A practical guide for Catholics*. The Catholic Truth
    Society, London, 2008, especially Chapter 9.